# The White Horse

# The White Horse
as described in the Book of Revelation, Chapter 19

by Emanuel Swedenborg

The Swedenborg Society
20-21 Bloomsbury Way
London WC1A 2TH

2007

All rights reserved. No part of this publication may be reproduced, stored in a retrieval system, or transmitted, in any form or by any means, without the prior permission in writing of The Swedenborg Society, or as expressly permitted by law, or under terms agreed with the appropriate reprographics rights organization. Enquiries concerning reproduction outside the scope of the above should be sent to The Swedenborg Society, at the address below. The author's moral rights have been asserted.

Published by:
The Swedenborg Society
Swedenborg House
20-21 Bloomsbury Way
London WC1A 2TH

© 2007, The Swedenborg Society

Preface and Translation: K C Ryder

Typeset at Swedenborg House.
Printed and bound in Great Britain
at the University Press, Cambridge.

Book Design: Stephen McNeilly

ISBN 978-0-85448-148-4
British Library Cataloguing-in-Publication Data.
A Catalogue record for this book is available
from the British Library.

# Contents

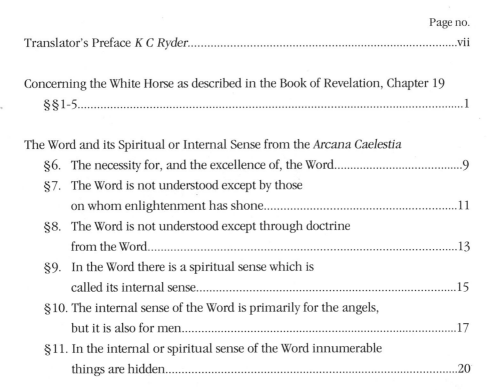

                                                                                                             Page no.

Translator's Preface *K C Ryder*......................................................................................vii

Concerning the White Horse as described in the Book of Revelation, Chapter 19
    §§1-5..................................................................................................................1

The Word and its Spiritual or Internal Sense from the *Arcana Caelestia*
    §6.  The necessity for, and the excellence of, the Word........................................9
    §7.  The Word is not understood except by those
           on whom enlightenment has shone..........................................................11
    §8.  The Word is not understood except through doctrine
           from the Word.........................................................................................13
    §9.  In the Word there is a spiritual sense which is
           called its internal sense............................................................................15
    §10. The internal sense of the Word is primarily for the angels,
           but it is also for men...............................................................................17
    §11. In the internal or spiritual sense of the Word innumerable
           things are hidden.....................................................................................20

§12. The Word has been written through correspondences, and thus through representative ideas...........................................23
§13. The literal or external sense of the Word...................................27
§14. The Lord is the Word......................................................................29
§15. Concerning those who are opposed to the Word........................31
§16. The Books which are indeed of the Word....................................32
§17. More about the Word.....................................................................33

Translator's Endnotes..............................................................................35
Index..........................................................................................................39

# Translator's Preface

The mere facts of Swedenborg's life and works are well documented and —at least by some people—well known. There is an excellent brief account, for example, in *The Oxford Companion to English Literature*.[1] Suffice to say here that he was born in Stockholm in 1688, the son of a pastor, and studied widely at Uppsala, Utrecht, Paris, and elsewhere (including a visit to the Bodleian Library in Oxford). In his youth he showed unusual brilliance in scientific matters, and later became an authority on natural science, natural philosophy, and engineering subjects.

He was also a prolific writer, and an inventor of note—an ear-trumpet at one end of the scale, and a device for transporting warships overland at the other. After his death it was found that much attributed to later scientists was actually due to him, his experimental work in aviation being an example. But it is his work post-1745, the year in which he received a divine commission to interpret the spiritual meaning of the Scriptures, for which he is chiefly remembered.

*De Equo Albo* was first published in London in 1758. It is an interpretation and expositon of the significance of *The White Horse as described in the Book of Revelation, Chapter 19*, and then an account of its spiritual sense from Swedenborg's *Arcana*

---

[1] OUP, 6th edition, 2000.

*Caelestia*. John Elliott, in his Preface to the 2004 Latin edition of the text, helpfully adds, 'No explicit reasons were provided by Swedenborg himself for the publication of this slender volume. Yet it may surely be assumed that it was intended to be a kind of brochure serving as an introduction to this magnum opus', i.e., *Arcana Caelestia*; to be read, we may reasonably conjecture, by the educated minority in the 18th century Protestant world, but specifically by the clergy caring for the souls of the uneducated, innumerate, and illiterate majority.

In preparing this translation I have been aware of earlier excellent work done in this field. I am also grateful for the help and advice of the Advisory and Revision Board of the Swedenborg Society, and their Publications Manager Stephen McNeilly; my brother the Revd Norman Ryder; but most of all the Revd John Elliott for his advice, common sense, knowledge of the topic, and considerable tact. If there are any mistakes, incidentally, they are mine.

I have tried to be sensitive to current ideas, outlook, and practice. This has meant that sometimes I have had to go all round the Wrekin, as it were, to express basically straighforward expressions or concepts in an acceptable way for today's reader. For instance we may no longer say that 'man was born for Heaven': we now say 'The human race was born for heaven' with a small 'h'. Again in this respect, if there are mistakes, they are mine. My guiding aim has been to produce a version which is readable and readily understandable for a 21st century readership while staying faithful to the nuances and progressions of Swedenborg's thoughts. I hope my aim has been true.

K C Ryder, Alton, March 2005

# The White Horse

# CONCERNING THE WHITE HORSE
## as described in the Book of Revelation, Chapter 19

1. In the writings of John, in the Book of Revelation, the following is a description of the Word in its spiritual sense, in other words the sense contained within it, or its 'inner meaning':

I saw heaven standing open, and behold, a White Horse. And the one sitting on the White Horse was called faithful and true, judging and fighting in righteousness. His eyes were a flame of fire, and on His head were many jewels. He had a name inscribed that no one knew but He Himself. And He was dressed in a garment dyed with blood, and His name is called the Word of God. The armies that followed Him in heaven were on white horses, they themselves dressed in clean white linen. On His garment and on His thigh was written a name, King of Kings and Lord of Lords. 19:11-14, 16.

No one can have a clear idea of what each of the details in this description entails except by way of its 'inner meaning'. It is obvious that each particular detail must represent or signify something, as follows:

Heaven which was standing open; a horse which was white; the one seated on it was called faithful and true,[1] judging and fighting in righteousness; His eyes a flame of fire; and many jewels[2] on His head; having a name inscribed that no one knew but He Himself; and dressed in a garment dyed with blood; and the armies that followed Him in heaven were on white horses, they themselves dressed in clean white linen;[3] on His garment and on His thigh He has written a name.

It is stated plainly that the one seated on the White Horse is the Word, and He is the Lord who is the Word, for what is said is that His name is called The Word of God; and then, He has written on His garment and on His thigh the title King of Kings and Lord of Lords.

From the interpretation of each individual phrase or statement it is clear that all this serves to describe the spiritual sense or internal meaning of the Word. The phrase 'heaven which was standing open' represents and signifies that the inner meaning of the Word is seen by those in heaven, and consequently also by those on earth for whom heaven stands open. 'A horse which was white' represents and signifies an understanding of the Word as regards its inner meanings.[4] That the 'white horse' means what I have said will be clear from what follows.

It is clear that 'the one seated on it' means the Lord in His capacity as the Word, and thus means the Word itself, for it is stated that 'His name is called the Word of God'; and he is called 'faithful' and 'judging in righteousness' because of His goodness; and 'true' and 'fighting in righteousness' because of His truth, for the Lord Himself is righteousness. 'His eyes a flame of fire' signify divine truth radiating from the divine good flowing from His divine love. The 'many jewels on His head' signify all the good and true properties of faith. Having a 'name written which no one knew other than He Himself' signifies that no one sees what is the nature of the Word in its inner meaning except Himself, and one to whom He reveals it.

'Dressed in a garment dyed with blood' signifies the violence done to the Word in its literal meaning.[5] 'The armies in heaven which followed Him on white horses' signifies those who understand the Word as regards its inner meanings.[6] 'Those dressed in clean white linen' signifies the same people who are endued with truth arising from what is good. 'On His garment and on His thigh a name written' signifies what is true and what is good and their specific qualities.

From all these verses, and from those which come before and after them, it is clear that they serve to foretell that the spiritual or internal sense of the Word will be laid open at around the final time of the Church; and what will happen at that time is also described there, Revelation 19: 17-21. There is no need to show here the things which are signified by these words since they are individually shown in *Arcana Caelestia*. The Lord is the Word because He is the divine truth: §§2533, 2803, 2894, 5272, 8535;[7] the Word is the divine truth: §§4692, 5075, 9987; He is proclaimed to be sitting on a horse judging and fighting in righteousness because the Lord is righteousness. The Lord is proclaimed to be righteousness from the fact that by His own power He has saved the human race: §§1813, 2025-2027, 9715, 9809, 10019, 10152. Righteousness is a merit belonging to the Lord alone: §§9715, 9979. 'His eyes a flame of fire' signify divine truth radiating from the divine good flowing from His divine love, because 'eyes' signify the understanding and truth of faith: §§2701, 4403-4421, 4523-4534, 6923, 9051, 10569; and 'a flame of fire' signifies the good of love: §§934, 4906, 5215, 6314, 6832; the 'jewels on His head'[8] signify all the good and true properties of faith: §§114, 3858, 6335, 6640, 9863, 9865, 9868, 9873, 9905.

'Having a name written which no one knew other than He Himself' signifies that no one sees what is the nature of the Word in its inner meaning except Himself, and one to whom He reveals it, because a name signifies the nature of a thing: §§144-145, 1754, 1896, 2009, 2724, 3006, 3237, 3421, 6674, 9310. 'Dressed in a garment dyed with blood' signifies the violence done to the Word in its literal meaning because 'a garment' signifies truth, which clothes what is good: §§1073, 2576, 5248, 5319, 5954, 9212, 9216, 9952, 10536; especially truth in its outermost form, and thus the Word in its literal meaning: §§5248, 6918, 9158, 9212; and because 'blood' signifies violence done to truth by what is false: §§374, 1005, 4735, 5476, 9127. 'The armies in heaven which followed Him on white horses' signify those who understand the Word as regards its inner meanings because 'armies' signify those who are equipped with the truth and goodness of heaven and the Church: §§3448, 7236, 7988, 8019; and 'the horse' signifies understanding: §§3217, 5321, 6125, 6400, 6534, 7024, 8146, 8381; and 'white' means the truth which the light of heaven has within itself—thus, the inner truth: §§3301, 3993, 4007, 5319.

'Those dressed in clean white linen' signify the same people who are endued with truth arising from what is good because 'linen' or 'a garment of linen' signifies truth from a heavenly source—which is truth from what is good: §§5319, 9469. 'On His garment and on His thigh a name written' signifies what is true and what is good, and their specific qualities, because 'a garment' signifies truth, and 'a name' signifies its nature, as above, and 'thigh' signifies the good properties of love: §§3021, 4277, 4280, 9961, 10488. 'King of Kings and Lord of Lords' is the Lord as regards divine truth and divine good; the Lord is called King by virtue of His divine truth: §§3009, 5068, 6148, and He is called Lord by virtue of His divine good: §§4973, 9167, 9194.

From all this it is clear what the nature of the Word is in its spiritual or inner sense, and that there is no single word within it which does not have some spiritual meaning relating to heaven and the Church.

2. In the prophetical parts of the Word a horse is mentioned very often,[9] but until now no one has known 'horse' means understanding, and 'horseman' one who understands, perhaps because it seems extraordinary and astonishing that that is what is meant by 'horse' in a spiritual sense, and consequently in the Word. But that it constantly means this can be agreed from very many instances in the Word, from which I should like to refer to only a few at this point.

In Israel's prophetic utterance[10] about Dan we find:

Dan will be a serpent on the road, a darting snake[11] on the path, that will bite the horse's heels, and the horseman will fall backwards. Genesis 49:17,18.

What this prophetic statement about one of the tribes of Israel means no one is going to understand unless he knows what 'serpent' signifies, and also 'horse' and 'horseman'. Yet is there anyone who does not see that it holds something spiritual within it? This being so, what the individual details signify may be seen in *Arcana Caelestia*, §§6398-6401, where this prophetical utterance is explained. In Habakkuk we find:

> O Lord [...] You ride on Your horses and Your chariots are salvation [...] You caused Your horses to tread in the sea. Habakkuk 3:8,15.

It is obvious that 'horses' here signify something spiritual, because these things are being said about God. What else would it be, 'God rode on [his] horses, and caused [his] horses to tread in the sea'? In Zechariah we find, with a similar significance:

> On that day, HOLY TO THE LORD will be on the horse-bells. Zechariah 14:20.[12]

In the same authority:

> On that day I will strike every horse with bewilderment and the horseman with madness—declares the Lord—I will open my gaze on the house of Judah, and I will strike with blindness every horse of the peoples. Zechariah 12:4,5.

What is being talked about here is the Church when it has been laid waste, which happens when there is no longer an understanding of anything true. This is what is being indicated by 'horse' and 'horseman'; what else would it be, '[...] every horse about to be struck with bewilderment [...] and the horse of the peoples with blindness'? What, otherwise, would this have to do with the Church?

In Job we find:

> Because God has made her[13] forget wisdom, neither has He imparted to her understanding; having raised herself on high, she mocks the horse and its rider. Job 39:17-19 ff.

That understanding is signified here by 'horse' is manifestly obvious; similarly in

David, where the expression 'to ride upon the word of truth' is used, Psalm 45:5; and besides in very many other places.

Moreover, who is likely to know why it is that Elijah and Elisha were called 'the chariots of Israel and its horsemen'; and why there appeared to Elisha's servant a mountain full of horses and fiery chariots, unless it is known what 'chariots' and 'horsemen' signify, and what Elijah and Elisha represented? For Elisha said to Elijah, 'My father, my father, the chariots of Israel and its horsemen', 2 Kings 2:11, 12; and King Joash said to Elisha, 'My father, my father [...] the chariots of Israel and its horsemen', 2 Kings 13:14. Concerning the servant of Elisha we read:

> The Lord opened the eyes of Elisha's servant, and he looked and saw the mountain full of horses and fiery chariots all around Elisha. 2 Kings 6:17.

Elijah and Elisha were called the chariots of Israel and its horsemen because each represented the Lord in his capacity as the Word. 'Chariots' represent doctrine derived from the Word, and 'horsemen' represent understanding. That Elijah and Elisha represented the Lord in this capacity may be seen in *Arcana Caelestia*: §§5247, 7643, 8029, 9327, and that 'chariots' signify doctrine derived from the Word: §§5321, 8215.

3. That 'horse' signifies understanding comes from no other source than from representatives in the spiritual world; horses are seen there very often, and those seated on horses, and even chariots, and everyone knows there that they signify things of the intellect and doctrine. It seemed to me quite often, when any there were thinking by using their own understanding of things, that they appeared as if they were riding on horses; this was how their meditating presented itself before others, though they themselves were unaware of it. There is also a place there where many come together who, using their own understanding of things, think and talk about the truths contained in doctrine; and when others come there they see that whole plain full of chariots and horses; and newcomers, who wonder where all this comes from, are taught that this is a manifestation resulting from their own intellectual thought; this place is called the Assembly of the Intelligent and Wise. There even appeared to me horses beaming

with light and chariots of fire, when certain souls were taken up into heaven, which was a sign that they were at that time instructed in the truths contained in heavenly doctrine, and made intelligent, and thus were taken up. As a result of my seeing this, there came into my mind what was signified by the chariot of fire and the horses of fire by which Elijah was taken up into heaven; and also by the horses and chariots of fire seen by Elisha's servant when his eyes were opened.

4. The fact that chariots and horses signified such things was very well known in the ancient churches, since those churches were representative churches;[14] and among those who were in them the knowledge of correspondences and representations was foremost among the branches of knowledge. From those churches the significance of 'horse'—that is, understanding—was passed around to the wise, even into Greece. From that they had the habit, when referring to their sun, where they located the god of their wisdom and understanding, of attributing to him a chariot and four fiery horses. And when they referred to their god of the sea, because by 'the sea' were signified those branches of knowledge which come as the result of understanding, they also attributed to him horses. And when they referred to the origin of the branches of knowledge as from the understanding, they figured a winged horse, which broke open a fountain with its hoof, at which were nine virgins—the branches of knowledge! For from the time of the ancient churches they knew that 'the horse' signified understanding, its 'wings' spiritual truth, its 'hoof' proper knowledge derived from the understanding, and 'the fountain' doctrine, which the branches of knowledge drew from. By the Trojan Horse nothing else is signified apart from a stratagem, from their own understanding, for destroying the walls. Even today, when understanding is referred to after the manner derived from those ancient folk, it is usually referred to as a flying horse—that is, Pegasus; doctrine is referred to as a fountain, and the branches of knowledge as virgins; but hardly anyone recognizes that 'horse' in its mystic sense signifies understanding, and even less that these significances were passed down from the ancient representative churches to the gentiles.

5. Since 'the White Horse' signifies the understanding of the Word as regards its spiritual

or internal sense, there will now follow all that has been revealed in *Arcana Caelestia* about the Word and that sense, for it is there that all things contained in Genesis and Exodus are explained according to the spiritual or internal sense of the Word.

# The Word and its Spiritual or Internal Sense from the *Arcana Caelestia*[15]

## 6. The necessity for, and the excellence of, the Word

In the dim light[16] of the natural order of things nothing may be known about the Lord, or about heaven and hell, or about the life of a person after death, or about the divine truths through which a person has spiritual and eternal life; see §§8944, 10318-10320. This may be agreed from the fact that many men, and scholars among them, do not believe these things, even though they are born where the Word is, and through it are instructed about these things: §10319. It was necessary therefore for there to be some revelation from heaven, because the human race was born for heaven: §1775. There has therefore been a revelation in every age: §2895, and there have been various types of revelation on this earth, one after another: §§10355, 10632. There was instant revelation for the most ancient peoples, who lived before the Flood, whose era was called the Golden Age, and therefore divine truth was inscribed upon their hearts: §2896. The Word was historical and prophetical for the ancient churches[17] who came after the Flood: §§2686, 2897. Details concerning these churches may be seen in *The New Jerusalem and Its [Heavenly] Doctrine*: §247. The historical parts of the Word were called The Wars of Jehovah, and the prophetical parts The Pronouncements: §2897. That Word was similar to our Word as regards inspiration, but adapted for those churches: §2897. It was mentioned by Moses: §§2686, 2897. But that Word was completely lost: §2897. There were also prophetical revelations amongst other peoples, as appears from the prophecies of Balaam: §2898. The Word is divine in all its single parts; see §§639, 680, 10321, 10637. The Word is divine and holy down to the last jot and tittle,[18] as has been demonstrated to me by an experience:[19] §1870. How it is explained today that the Word is inspired down to the last jot: §1886.

The Church exists in particular where the Word is, and through it the Lord is known, and the divine truths revealed: §§3857, 10761. But indeed those who are born where the Word is, and where through the Word the Lord is known, are not simply by that very reason of the Church: those people are of the Church who are given rebirth by the Lord through the truths from the Word, who live according to the truths there, so, those who live a life of love and faith: §§6637, 10143, 10153, 10578, 10645, 10829.

## 7. The Word is not understood except by those on whom enlightenment has shone

The human intellect cannot grasp divine ideas, nor even spiritual ones, unless it is enlightened by the Lord: §§2196, 2203, 2209, 2654. In this way only the enlightened grasp the Word: §10323. The Lord grants to those who are enlightened understanding of truths, and discernment of things which appear to contradict one another: §§9382, 10659. The Word in its literal sense may not be consistent with itself, and often appears to contradict itself: §9025. For that very reason it can be explained and interpreted by the unenlightened in order to confirm any opinion and heresy whatsoever, and to provide a justification for any earthly and bodily love whatsoever: §§4783, 10330, 10400. Those who read the Word from a love of truth and goodness are enlightened by the Word, but not those who read it from a love of fame, gain, honour, or indeed a love of self: §§9382, 10548-10551. Those who lead a life of good and so have an affection for the truth are enlightened: §8694. Those whose internal self is opened may be enlightened, and so they can be raised to the light of heaven as regards the internal man: §§10400, 10402, 10691, 10694. Enlightenment is an actual opening of the interior parts of the mind, and also a raising into the light of heaven: §10330. Holiness from the internal self, that is, from the Lord through the internal self, flows into those who hold the Word sacred, even when they do not know it: §6789. Those people are enlightened, and see truths in the Word, who are led by the Lord, but not those who are led by themselves: §10638.

Those are led by the Lord who love truth because it is the truth, who also love to lead a life according with divine truths: §§10578, 10645, 10829. The Word is brought to life for a person in the same measure that a life of love and faith resides in that person: §1776. Things which come from a person's own personal understanding have no life in themselves, because nothing good derives from a person's own properties: §§8941, 8944. Those who have confirmed themselves in large measure in false doctrine cannot be enlightened: §10640.

It is the understanding which is enlightened: §§6608, 9300. It is the understanding which is a recipient of the truth: §§6222, 6608, 10659. Regarding every doctrinal point of the Church, there are ideas from the understanding and so from thought, according to which the doctrinal point is perceived: §§3310, 3825. The ideas of a person, as long as he or she lives on earth, are natural, because then a person thinks on the natural level; but further, spiritual ideas are concealed in people, at least among those who have affection for the truth because it is the truth; and a person comes to these ideas after death: §§3310, 5510, 6201, 10237, 10240, 10551. Without ideas from the understanding and so from thought there is no perception about any thing at all: §3825. Ideas about matters of faith are revealed in the next life, and there they are seen as they truly are by the angels, and a person is then linked to other ideas, as far as those ideas proceed from an affection belonging to love: §§1869, 3310, 5510, 6200, 6201, 8885. For that reason the Word is not understood other than by a person who sees truth in God's light; for to believe something without an idea of that thing and without any such insight of it is just to retain in the memory an utterance devoid of all life of perception and affection, which is [the same as] not believing: §2553. It is the literal sense of the Word which is enlightened: §§3436, 9824, 9905, 10548.

## 8. The Word is not understood except through doctrine from the Word

The doctrine of the Church must be from the Word: §§3464, 5402, 5432, 10763, 10764. Doctrine without the Word is not understood: §§9025, 9409, 9424, 9430, 10324, 10431, 10584. True doctrine is a lantern to those who read the Word: §10400. True doctrine must be derived from those [20] who have received enlightenment from the Lord: §§2510, 2516, 2519, 9424, 10105. The Word is understood through doctrine formed by one who is enlightened: §10324. Those who have received enlightenment form doctrine for themselves from the Word: §§9382, 10659. There is a difference between those who teach and learn from the doctrine of the Church, and those who do this from the literal sense of the Word alone; and what that difference is: §9025. Those who rely on the literal sense of the Word and are without doctrine reach no understanding about divine truths: §§9409-9410, 10582. They fall into many errors: §10431. When those who have affection for the truth because it is the truth become adult and can see with their own understanding, they do not simply remain in the doctrinal ideas of their own Church but find out for themselves from the Word whether they are true: §§5402, 5432, 6047. Otherwise anyone's idea of the truth would be derived from someone else and from the land of their birth, whether Jew or Greek: §6047. Still, things that have become items of faith from the literal sense of the Word must not be extinguished except after full examination: §9039.

The true doctrine of the Church is the doctrine of love, in the sense of affectionate regard for your fellow man,[21] and faith: §§2417, 4766, 10763-10764. The doctrine of faith does not make the Church, but a life of faith does, which is love: §§809, 1798-1799, 1834, 4468, 4672, 4766, 5826, 6637. Doctrinal ideas are nothing unless life is lived according to them; and everyone can see that they exist for the sake of life, and not for the sake of memory, and then for a degree of thought: §§1515, 2049, 2116. In the various national churches today there is a doctrine of faith and not of love, and the doctrine of love has been driven backwards into a branch of learning, called Moral Theology: §2417. The Church would be a united whole if people were recognized as being people of the Church by the life they lead and the love they show: §§1285, 1316, 2982, 3267, 3445, 3451-3452. How much a doctrine of love is worth compared with a doctrine of faith divorced from love: §4844. Those who know nothing of love are in ignorance of heavenly things: §2435. Those who have only a doctrine of faith and not of love slide into lost ways, on which subject see §§2383, 2417, 3146, 3325, 3412-3413, 3416, 3773, 4672, 4730, 4783, 4925, 5351, 7623-7627, 7752-7762, 7790, 8094, 8313, 8530, 8765, 9186, 9224, 10555. Those who exist only in the doctrine of faith, and not in the life of faith, which is love, were in other times called the Uncircumcised, or Philistines: §§3412-3413, 3463, 8093, 8313, 9340. Among the ancients there was a doctrine of love towards the Lord, and love in the sense of affectionate regard towards your neighbour, and the doctrine of faith was subordinate to this: §§2417, 3419, 4844, 4955.

Doctrine formed by one who is enlightened can later be substantiated by rational proofs and proofs founded on sound knowledge, and in this way it can be more fully understood, and corroborated: §§2553, 2719, 2720, 3052, 3310, 6047. More on this topic may be seen in *The New Jerusalem and Its [Heavenly] Doctrine*, §51. Those who live in faith divorced from love would wish the doctrinal ideas of the Church to be believed simply, without any rational consideration: §3394.

A man who is wise does not just uphold a dogma but sees whether it is true before he upholds it, and this does happen among those who are in a state of enlightenment: §§1017, 4741, 7012, 7680, 7950. This enlightenment is natural, not spiritual, and achievable even among the wicked: §8780. Everything, even falsehoods, can be upheld, even to the extent that they appear to be truths: §§2482, 2490, 5033, 6865, 8521.

## 9. In the Word there is a spiritual sense which is called its internal sense

No one can know what is the spiritual or internal sense of the Word unless he knows what correspondence is: §§2895, 4322. Every single thing which is in the natural world, right down to the very least thing, corresponds to something spiritual, and so signifies it: §§1886-1889, 2987-3003, 3213-3227. Spiritual things, to which the natural things correspond, appear in nature under another guise, with the result that they are not recognized: §§1887, 2395, 8920. Hardly anyone knows where divine quality is in the Word, though it is there in its internal or spiritual sense, the existence of which is not known today: §§2899, 4989.

What lies hidden in the Word is nothing other than what its internal or spiritual sense contains, in which the Lord, the glorification of His human form, His kingdom, and His Church are dealt with, and not natural things, which are of the world: §4923. In very many places the prophetical elements are not understood, and so are of no benefit, without the internal sense—from examples in §§2608, 8020, 8398—just as what is signified by the White Horse in the Book of Revelation, from §§2760 ff. What is meant by the Keys of the Kingdom of Heaven given to Peter: Preface to Genesis 22, and §9410. What is meant by flesh, blood, bread, and wine in the Holy Supper: §8682. What is meant by the prophecies of Jacob concerning his sons: Genesis 49, and §§6306, 6333-6465. What is meant by many other prophecies about Judah and Israel which do not match with [aspects of] that nation, and do not coincide with one another in their literal sense: §§6333, 6361, 6415, 6438, 6444. In addition there are very many others: §2608. Further, what is said about correspondence may be seen in the work *Heaven and Hell*, §§87-115, 303-310.

Concerning the internal or spiritual sense of the Word in general: §§1767-1777, 1869-1879. There is an internal sense in every single part of the Word: §§1143, 1984, 2135, 2333, 2395, 2495, 2619. These ideas do not appear in the literal sense but still they are in it: §4442.

## 10. The internal sense of the Word is primarily for the angels, but it is also for men

So that it may be known what the internal sense is, its nature and its origin, this will be stated in summary form. They think and speak differently in heaven from people on earth—in heaven spiritually and on earth naturally. Therefore when people read the word the angels who are with them perceive it spiritually, and the people naturally. So, angels are in the spiritual sense, people in the external sense; and yet they still make one unit because there is a correspondence between them. Angels not only think spiritually, they also speak spiritually; also, their presence with people, and their conjunction with people is achieved through the Word. This is seen in the work *Heaven and Hell*, where the wisdom of the angels of heaven is considered: §§265-275; their speech: §§234-245; their connection with people: §§291-302; their connection through the Word: §§303-310.

The Word is understood differently by the angels in heaven and by people on earth; and an internal or spiritual sense exists for the angels, while for men there is an external or natural sense: §1887, 2395. The angels perceive the Word in its internal sense, not its external, from the experience of those from heaven who talked with me when I read the Word: §§1769-1772. Angelic ideas[22] and angelic speech are spiritual, while human ideas and speech are natural, and likewise the internal sense, which is spiritual, is for angels, as shown to me by my own experience: §2333. Nevertheless the literal sense of the Word[23] serves as a means of communicating the spiritual ideas of angels, in the same way that words of speech serve for the sense of a thing with people: §2143. Those things which belong to the internal sense of the Word fall into such things as are in the light of heaven, and so into the perception of angels: §§2618-2619, 2629, 3086. Likewise those things which the angels perceive from the Word are very precious to them: §§2540-2541, 2545, 2551. Angels understand not even one expression of the literal sense of the Word: §§64-65, 1434, 1929. Nor do they know the names of persons and places mentioned in the Word: §§1434, 1888, 4442, 4480. Names cannot enter heaven or be pronounced there: §§1876, 1888. All names in the Word signify spiritual realities, and in heaven they are converted into the ideas of spiritual reality: §§768, 1888, 4310, 4442, 5225, 5287, 10329. Also, angels abstract spiritual realities from people and their names: §§4380, 8343, 8985, 9007. How elegant the internal sense of the Word is, even where no names occur, is seen in examples from the Word: §§1224, 1888, 2395. Also, several names in succession express one thing in the internal sense: §5095. Also, all numbers in the Word signify things: §§482, 487, 647-648, 755, 813, 1963, 1988, 2075, 2252, 3252, 4264, 6175, 9488, 9659, 10217, 10253. Spirits too perceive the Word in its internal sense, in so far as their internal parts are opened to heaven: §1771. The literal sense of the Word, which is natural, may be transmuted in a moment of time into spiritual form among the angels, because correspondence exists: §5648. And this is without their hearing or knowing what is in the literal or external sense: §10215. Thus, the literal or external sense exists only with man and progresses no further: §2015.

There is an internal sense of the Word, and also an innermost or supreme sense, about which see §§9407, 10604, 10614, 10627. The spiritual angels, that is those who are in the Lord's spiritual kingdom, perceive the Word in its internal sense, and the celestial angels, who are in the Lord's celestial kingdom, perceive the Word in its innermost sense: §§2157, 2275.

The Word is for people and also for angels, being appropriate for both: §§7381, 8862, 10322. It is the Word which unifies heaven and earth: §§2310, 2495, 9212, 9216, 9357. The linking of heaven with people exists through the Word: §§9396, §9400-9401, 10452. The Word is called a covenant [contract]: §9396—since a covenant signifies a linking together: §§665-666, 1023, 1038, 1864, 1996, 2003, 2021, 6804, 8767, 8778, 9396, 10632. There is an internal sense of the Word because the Word came down[24] from the Lord through the three heavens right as far as humans: §§2310, 6597. It has become appropriate for the angels of the three heavens and also for humans: §§7381, 8862. It is from this that the Word is divine: §§4989, 9280, and holy: §10276, and spiritual: §4480, and inspired by the Divine: §9094. That is inspiration: §9094.

Furthermore, people who have been regenerated are actually in the internal sense of the Word even though they do not know this, since their internal being is opened, which has spiritual perception: §10400. But in their case the spiritual essence of the Word flows into natural ideas and is thus established in a natural sense, since while they live in the world they think as natural beings, as far as perception is concerned: §5614. The light of truth among those who are enlightened comes from their internal being, and thus through their internal being from the Lord: §§10691, 10694. Also along that course flows what is holy, among those who hold the Word holy: §6789. Since regenerated people are actually in the internal sense of the Word, and in its holiness, although they do not know that, after death they arrive at that of themselves, and are no longer in the literal sense: §§3226, 3342-3343. The ideas of an internal person are spiritual, but while people live in the world they are not aware of them since people are in their natural mode of thought, to which they impart their reasoning faculty: §§10236, 10240, 10551. But after death people come into them as their own because they belong properly to their spirit, and at that time they not only think but also talk as from them: §§2470, 2472, 2476, 10568, 10604. It is for this reason that it is said that regenerated people do not know that they are in the spiritual sense of the Word, and that from this enlightenment comes to them.

## 11. In the internal or spiritual sense of the Word innumerable things are hidden

The Word in its internal sense contains many things which surpass human comprehension: §§3085-3086. They cannot be expressed in words, and cannot be explained: §1955. They exist solely for the angels, and are understood by them: §167. The internal sense of the Word contains the hidden things of heaven, which have to do with the Lord and His kingdom in heaven and on earth: §§1-4, 937. Those hidden things do not appear in the literal sense: §§937, 1502, 2161. Many other things in the writings of the prophets, which appear as if randomly scattered, in the internal sense fit together continuously in a beautiful[25] sequence: §7153, 9022. In its original language not a single word, not even a single jot, can be missing from the literal meaning without interruption of the internal sense; and for that very reason the Word, out of the Lord's divine providence, has been preserved so completely, down to the last title: §7933. There are innumerable things in each individual part of the Word: §§6617, 6620, 8920. And in each and every phrase: §1869. Countless things are contained in the Lord's Prayer and in its individual petitions: §6619. And in the Ten Commandments; though in the external sense of these there are some ideas which are known to every nation without revelation: §§8862, 8899. In every tiny little tittle of a letter of the Word in its original language there is something holy, revealed from Heaven—this may be seen in the work *Heaven and Hell*, §260, where the words of the Lord are explained, that Not one jot or tittle shall be lost from the Law; Matthew 5:18.

Particularly in the prophetical part of the Word there are two expressions of the same thing, as it were, but one refers to what is good and the other to what is true: §§683, 707, 2576, 8339. In the Word things relating to what is good and what is true are married together, to an amazing degree, but that marriage is evident only to one who is acquainted with the internal sense: §10554. So, in the Word and in its individual parts there are divine marriage and heavenly marriage: §§683, 793, 801, 2173, 2516, 2712, 5138, 7022. Divine marriage, which is the marriage between divine good and divine truth, is thus the Lord in heaven, in whom alone that marriage exists there: §§3004-3005, 3009, 4137, 5194, 5502, 6343, 7945, 8339, 9263, 9314. Through Jesus also there is signified divine good, and through Christ divine truth, and thus through both divine marriage in heaven is signified: §§3004-3005, 3009. This marriage—and thus the Lord as regards divine good and divine truth—is in each individual part of the Word in its internal sense: §5502. The marriage of good and truth by the Lord in heaven and in the Church is what is called heavenly marriage: §§2508, 2618, 2803, 3004, 3211, 3952, 6179. Thus in this respect the Word is heaven, so to speak: §§2173, 10126. Heaven is likened to marriage in the Word from the marriage of good and truth there: §§2758, 3132, 4434, 4835. The internal sense is itself the genuine doctrine of the Church: §§9025, 9430, 10400. Those who understand the Word according to its internal sense know the true doctrine itself of the Church, because the internal sense contains that: §§9025, 9430, 10400. The internal part of the Word is also the internal part of the Church, and so also of worship: §10460. The Word is the doctrine of love towards the Lord, and affectionate regard for your neighbour: §§3419-3420.

The Word in its literal meaning is like a cloud, and its glory is in its internal sense —Preface to Genesis 18; also §§5922, 6343—where there is explained that the Lord will come in the clouds of the sky with glory. Also 'cloud' in the Word signifies the Word in its literal sense, and 'glory' signifies the Word in its internal sense—Preface to Genesis 18: also §§4060, 4391, 5922, 6343, 6752, 8106, 8781, 9430, 10551, 10574. Things which are in the literal sense, compared to those in the internal sense, are like rough projections round a polished optical cylinder, from which nevertheless there exists in the cylinder a beautiful image of a man: §1871. Those who wish for and recognize only the literal sense are represented in the spiritual world as an ugly little old woman, while those who wish for and recognize at the same time the internal sense appear as a virgin finely clothed: §1774. The Word in all that it embraces is an image of heaven, because the Word is divine truth, and divine truth constitutes heaven, and heaven resembles one human, and in that respect The Word is an image of a human, as it were: §1871. That heaven in its total make-up resembles one human may be seen in the work *Heaven and Hell*: §§59-67. That divine truth proceeding from the Lord constitutes heaven, *Heaven and Hell*: §§126-140, 200-212. The Word is presented to the Angels in a beautiful and delightful way: §§1767-1768. The literal sense is like a body, and the internal sense is like the soul of that body: §8943.

Consequently, life for the Word comes from its internal sense: §§1405, 4857. The Word is pure in its internal sense, and it does not appear so in its literal sense: §§2362, 2395. Things in the literal sense become holy from internal things: §§10126, 10276. In the historical narratives of the Word also there is an internal sense, but within them: §4989. Thus the historical parts just as much as the prophetical parts contain hidden things of heaven: §§755, 1659, 1709, 2310, 2333. The angels perceive these not in relation to history but in relation to doctrine, because they perceive them spiritually: §6884. The innermost hidden things in the historical narratives are less evident to humans than those in the prophetical parts for the simple reason that their minds are intent upon, and in contemplation of, the historical parts: §§2176, 6597.

Moreover, the nature of the internal sense of the Word is shown: §§1756, 1984, 2004, 2663, 3035, 7089, 10604, 10614, and it is illustrated by comparisons: §1873.

## 12. The Word has been written through correspondences, and thus through representative ideas

The Word as regards its literal sense has been written through correspondences alone, and thus through such things as represent and signify the spiritual aspects of heaven and the Church: §§1404, 1408-1409, 1540, 1619, 1659, 1709, 1783, 2179, 2763, 2899. This was done because of the internal sense in each particular instance: §2899; thus too for the sake of heaven, since those who are in heaven do not understand the Word according to its literal or natural sense but according to its internal, or spiritual sense: §2899. The Lord spoke through correspondences, through representative and signifying ideas, because He spoke from His divine being: §§9049, 9063, 9086, 10126, 10276. The Lord thus spoke directly to the world and at the same time to heaven: §§2533, 4807, 9049, 9063, 9086. Whatever the Lord spoke filled the whole of heaven:[26] §4637. The historical narratives of the Word are representative, and their actual words have significances: §§1540, 1659, 1709, 1783, 2686. The Word could not have been written in any other style for there to be communication through it with heaven: §§2899, 6943, 9401. Those who treat the Word with contempt because of its simple and seemingly uncultivated style, and think that they would accept it if it had been written in a different style, are greatly mistaken: §8783. Also, the manner and style of writing of the most ancient authors was through correspondences and representative ideas: §§605, 1756, 9942. I found through my own experience that the wise men of ancient times were delighted by the

Word, because they found there representative and significant ideas: §§2592-2593. If someone of the most ancient Church had read the Word, he would have seen clearly those things which are in the internal sense and obscurely those things in the external sense: §4493. The sons of Jacob were brought down into the land of Canaan because all places in that land were from very ancient times made representative: §§1585, 3686, 4447, 5136, 6516; and so that the Word might be written there, where places were to be named because of their internal meaning: §§3686, 4447, 5136, 6516. But in fact the Word in its external sense was altered on account of that people, though not as regards its internal sense: §§10453, 10461, 10603-10604. Many passages from the Word are quoted about that nation, which must however be understood according to their internal sense—that is, other than according to the literal sense: §7051. Since that nation represented the Church, and because the Word was written among and about that nation, therefore heavenly ideas were signified by their names, for example Reuben, Simeon, Levi, Judah, Ephraim, Joseph and the rest; and by Judah in the internal sense is signified the Lord as regards celestial love, and His heavenly kingdom: §§3654, 3881, 5583, 5782, §6362-6381.

So that it may be known what are the correspondences and their nature, and what is the nature of the representations in the Word, something will also be said about those. All things which correspond also represent and then signify something, such that correspondences and representations go together as one: §§2896, 2899, 2973, 2987, 2989-2990, 3002, 3225. What those correspondences and representations are, from my own experience and examples: §§2763, 2987-3002, 3213-3226, 3337-3352, §3472-3485, 4218-4228, 9280. The knowledge of correspondences and representations was the most important field of knowledge among the ancients: §§3021, 3419, 4280, 4749, 4844, 4964, 4966, 6004, 7729, 10252; especially among people in eastern parts: §§5702, 6692, 7097, 7779, 9391, 10252, 10407; in Egypt more than other places: §§5702, 6692, 7097, 7779, 9391, 10407; even among the Gentiles, for example in Greece and elsewhere: §§2762, 7729. But today it is among the lost fields of knowledge, especially in Europe: §§2894-2895, 2995, 3630, 3632, 3747-3749, 4581, 4966, 10252. But always that type of knowledge is more important than all others, since without it the Word is not understood; nor are the rites of the Jewish Church which are written about in the Word; nor is it known what the nature of heaven is, nor is it known what that which is spiritual is, nor how it happens that there is an inflowing of the spiritual into the natural, nor how there is an inflowing of the soul into the body, and many other things: §4280, and in passages cited above. All things which appear among spirits and angels are representative in accord with correspondences: §§1971, 3213-3226, 3475, 3485, 9457, 9481, 9576-9577. Heaven is full of representations: §§1521, 1532, 1619. Representations are more beautiful and perfect the more interior they are in heaven: §3475. Representations there are real appearances since they come from the light of heaven, which is the divine truth; and this itself is the essential part of all things that are in existence: §3485.

The reason why every single thing in the spiritual world is represented in the natural world is that what is internal clothes itself as appropriate in what is its external guise, through which it presents itself visibly, and becomes apparent: §§6275, 6284, 6299. Thus, an end clothes itself in suitable guises in order to present itself as a cause in a lower sphere, and then as an effect in a still lower sphere; and when an end passes by way of a cause into an effect, it presents itself visibly, or becomes apparent right before the eyes: §5711.

This is illustrated by the inflowing of the soul into the body: namely, the soul is clothed with such things in the body through which everything it thinks and wishes can present itself and become apparent visibly; therefore when thought flows down into the body it is represented by such gestures and actions as correspond to it: §2988. Quite clearly the feelings of the mind are represented in the face by its various expressions, to such an extent that they are seen there: §§4791-4805, 5695. From this it is plain that in every single thing within the natural order there lies hidden deep inside a cause and an end from the spiritual world: §§3562, 5711—since things which are in the natural order are final effects, within which are prior causes: §§4240, 4939, 5651, 6275, 6284, 6299, 9216. Whatever is internal is that which is represented, and what is external that which serves to represent it: §4292.

What correspondences and representations are may be further seen in the work *Heaven and Hell*, where the correspondence of all things of heaven with all human things is dealt with: §§87-102; the correspondence of heaven with all things of earth: §§103-115; and representations and appearances in heaven: §§170-176.

Since all things in the natural order are representative of spiritual and celestial realities, in ancient times there were churches in which all the external observances or rituals were representative: §§519, 521, 2896. The Church was set up among the children of Israel as a representative church: §§1003, 2179, 10149. There all the rituals were external forms representing the internal things of heaven and the Church: §§4288, 4874. The representative things of the Church and worship ceased when the Lord came into the world and manifested Himself, because the Lord revealed the internal things of the Church, and all things of that Church, in a supreme sense, had regard to Him: §4835.

## 13. The literal or external sense of the Word

The literal sense of the Word accords with appearances in the world: §§589, 926, 1832, 1874, 2242, 2520, 2533, §2719-2720, and is suited to the comprehension of the pure in heart: §§2533, 9049, 9063, 9086. The Word in its literal sense is natural, see §8783, because what is natural is the final thing upon which spiritual and celestial things come to rest, and upon which they stand like a house on its foundation; furthermore, an internal sense without an external form would be like a house without a foundation: §§9360, 9430, 9433, 9824, 10044, 10436. The Word, because that is its nature, is the container of a spiritual sense and a celestial sense: §9407. And because that is its nature, there is a divine holiness in the literal sense extending to every single detail, right down to the last jot: §§639, 680, 1869-1870, 9198, 10321, 10637. Although the laws laid down before the children of Israel have now been totally abrogated they are still the holy Word because of the internal sense in them: §§9211, 9259, 9349. The laws, judgements, and statutes laid down for the Israelite or Jewish Church, which was a representative church, are in some cases still valid in both senses, the external and the internal; some of them should be wholly observed according to their external sense; some may be of use if people wish; and some have been totally abrogated; about all these: §9349. The Word is divine even as regards those of the above which have been abrogated, because of the heavenly elements which are concealed in their internal sense: §10637.

What the nature of the Word is in its literal sense if it is not understood at the same time in its internal sense; or, expressed otherwise, according to the true doctrine from the Word: §10402. From the literal sense without the internal sense, or without genuine doctrine from the Word, a vast number of heresies comes gushing out: §10400. Those who live in external elements without internal elements cannot uphold the inner parts of the Word: §10694. Such were the Jews, and such are they today: §§301-303, 3479, 4429, 4433, 4680, 4844, 4847, 10396, 10401, 10407, 10694, 10705, 10707.

## 14. The Lord is the Word

In the innermost sense of the Word the only consideration is the Lord Himself, and all the states of the glorification of His human form are described; that is, of His union with the Divine Itself; and all the states in which He was bringing hell into subjection to Himself, imposing order on everything there, and in heaven also: §§2249, 7014. So, the whole life of the Lord in the world is described in that sense, and through the Word the presence of the Lord with the angels is continuous: §2523. Therefore the Lord alone is in the innermost part of the Word, and the divinity and sanctity of the Word derive from that: §§1873, 9357. The Lord's saying that the Scripture concerning Himself has been fulfilled means the fulfilment of all things in its innermost sense: §7933.

The Word means divine truth: §§4692, 5075, 9987. The Lord is the Word because He is the divine truth: §2533. The Lord is also the Word because it comes from Him and is about Him, see §2859, and about the Lord alone in the innermost sense, and thus the Lord Himself is there: §§1873, 9357. And because in every single part of the Word there is the marriage of divine good and divine truth, that marriage is in the Lord alone: §§3004-3005, 3009, 4138, 5194, 5502, 6343, 7945, 8339, 9263, 9314. The divine Word is the one and only reality, and that in which it is, which is from what is divine, is the only true essence: §§5272, 6880, 7004, 8200. And because the divine truth proceeding from the Lord, as from the sun in heaven, is the light there, and the divine good is the warmth there; and because all things there exist from these, just as everything in the world exists from light and warmth, which are also in their own essential substances and act through them; and because the natural world comes into being through heaven or the spiritual world; it is clear that all things which have been created were created from the divine truth, and so from the Word, according to these words from John: In the beginning was the Word, and the Word was with God, and the Word was God, and through it [27] all things were made that were made; and THE WORD WAS MADE FLESH; John 1: 1-3, 14 and §§2803, 2894, 5272, 7850. More about the creation of all things from the divine truth, and thus from the Lord, may be seen in the work *Heaven and Hell*: §137, and more fully in the section where there is a discussion of the sun in heaven, which is the Lord, and which is His divine love: §§116-125. And the divine truth is light, and the divine good is warmth from that same sun in heaven: §§126-140.

The linking of the Lord with man comes through the Word by means of its internal sense: §10375. This linking comes about through every single detail of the Word, and for this reason the Word is wonderful compared with everything ever written: §§10632-10634. Once the Word was written, the Lord spoke through it to people: §10290. In addition there may also be seen ideas raised in the work *Heaven and Hell* concerning the linking of heaven with people through the Word: §§303-310.

## 15. Concerning those who are opposed to the Word

Concerning those who mock, blaspheme against, and profane the Word: §1878. What is their quality in the other life: §§1761, 9222. What the vicious parts of the blood mean: §5719.[28] The degree of danger from profanation of the Word: §§571, 582. How harmful it is if false assumptions, especially those which promote love of self and worldly things, are confirmed through the Word: §589. Those who have no affection for the truth because it is the truth are quite clearly rejecting those things which belong to the internal sense of the Word, and are nauseated by them, based on my experience of such persons in the world of spirits: §5702. Certain persons in the other life who tried absolutely to reject the inner parts of the word were deprived of reason: §1879.

## 16. The Books which are indeed of the Word

The Books of the Word are all those which have an internal sense, while those which do not have this are not the Word. The Books of the Word in the Old Testament are the five Books of Moses; Joshua; Judges; the two Books of Samuel; the two Books of Kings; the Psalms of David; the prophets Isaiah, Jeremiah, Lamentations, Ezekiel, Daniel, Hosea, Joel, Amos, Obadiah, Jonah, Micah, Nahum, Habakkuk, Zephaniah, Haggai, Zechariah, Malachi; in the New Testament the four Evangelists—Matthew, Mark, Luke, John—and Revelation. The rest do not have an internal sense: §10325.

The Book of Job is an ancient book in which indeed there are elements of internal sense, but it is not continuous throughout: §§3540, 9942.

## 17. More about the Word

'Word' in the Hebrew language means various things, such as 'the spoken word', 'thought of the mind', 'every thing that really exists', and 'something': §9987. The Word signifies divine truth and the Lord: §§2533, 4692, 5075, 9987. Words signify truths: §§4692, 5075. They signify doctrinal ideas: §1288. The Ten Words[29] signify all divine truths: §10688.

There are two separate expressions for one thing in the Word, especially the prophetical parts; one relates to good, and the other to truth, and thus they are linked: §§683, 707, 2516, 8339. Which expression refers to good, and which to truth, cannot be known except from the internal sense of the Word, since there are particular terms by which things of the good are expressed, and others for things of the truth: §§793, 801. This is so much the case that simply from the terms used it may be known whether good or truth is being discussed: §2712. Again, at one time the one expression involves a general point, and the other involves a meaning determined from the general: §2212. There is a sort of reciprocity in the Word, concerning which see §2240. Most things in the Word also have an opposite sense: §4816. The internal sense is in accordance with its own subject, rather like a predicate: §4502.

Those who have been delighted by the Word receive the warmth of heaven in the other life, in which there is heavenly love, according to the quality and quantity of the delight they derive from love: §1773.

# Translator's Endnotes

| | |
|---|---|
| LS | Lewis and Short's *Latin Dictionary*. |
| MLW | Baxter and Johnson's *Medieval Latin Word-List*. |
| Elliott | From conversation and correspondence with the Revd John Elliott, consultant of this work and Editor of the 3rd Latin edition of *De Equo Albo* (2004) whose wisdom and clear insights have been much appreciated by the translator. |

1. Elliott: 'The [original Latin] text ought surely to read, as *Arcana Caelestia* §2760; *quod fidelis et verus, et in justitia* ...' The translator has followed this conjecture.
2. In translating *diademata* as 'jewels', rather than 'crowns', I have noted Elliott, who draws attention to John Chadwick's assertion (from his *Lexicon to the Latin Texts of Swedenborg's Theological Writings*), that there can be little doubt that Swedenborg understood jewel not crown by the Latin word *diadema*.
3. The Latin *byssinus* means 'a garment made from byssus' (LS). *Byssus*: cotton (MLW); cotton, or (according to some) a kind of flax, and the linen made from it (LS).
4. The Latin *interiora* (plural of *interius*, and comp. of *internum*) means 'inward' or 'internal' (LS). It may also signify: 'more hidden', 'secret' or 'unknown' (LS).
5. I am grateful to Elliott for the suggestion of translating *litera* as 'in its literal meaning'. I was in a fog as to Swedenborg's intention in using *litera*, which classically may mean either 'a letter' or 'writing'.
6. See note 4 above.
7. Throughout this translation I have used the reference numbers following the emendations made by Elliott in *De Equo Albo* (2004).

## Endnotes

[8] See note 2 above.

[9] The text has simply *equus* (horse) at this point, but there is a 'parallel passage' in *Arcana Caelestia* §2761, stating *equus et eques* (horse and horseman): the sense of what follows in the current passage suggests that Swedenborg intends *equus et eques* here.

[10] Elliott points out that 'Israel here of course means the patriarch Jacob'.

[11] Biblical translations are based on the Schmidt Latin translation (1696) as apparently used by Swedenborg, though here, as sometimes elsewhere, Swedenborg does misquote (in this case inserting *jaculus* after the second *serpens*). LS, always an interesting source, glosses *jaculus* as follows: 'sc. *serpens*, a serpent that darts from a tree on its prey'.

[12] Elliott: 'As I understand it, this is not a statement on the horse-bells to the effect that the bells are holy but that they ring out the holiness of things attributable to the Lord. (A bit like the bells rung in a catholic mass which draw the worshippers' attention to the just-consecrated host or wine that is being elevated.)'

[13] *her.* The Hebrew pronoun in Job 39:17, which refers to a bird, is feminine. Although Swedenborg rendered it *eum* (him) in *Arcana Caelestia* §2762 and here in *De Equo Albo*, *eam* (her) occurs in other places of his works where this verse is quoted.

[14] That is, these churches recognized that particular words and expressions represented particular ideas.

[15] The vast majority of Swedenborg's posits in this section are introduced with the Latin conjunction *quod*; I have dispensed with the equivalent English *that* in each case in order to ease fluent reading.

[16] Swedenborg uses *lumine* (from *lumen*) for 'light' here. Elliott helpfully points out that Swedenborg tends to use *lumen* when referring to light of inferior quality, reserving *lux* for light which is divinely inspired.

[17] *De Nova Hierosolyma* (NH) has *in antiquis...*; *De Equo Albo* has no *in*, and I have translated it as a dative case 'for'.

[18] Elliott points out that 'tittle' does not appear in the modern English version of the New Testament, and suggests replacing it with 'small part'; but 'tittle' is such a lovely little word, and besides has for me strong redolences of biblical readings ringing in my childhood ears, that I have decided to keep it. Tittle is in fact the mark or dot over the letter i, i.e., jot.

[19] I am grateful for Elliott's advice that 'Swedenborg is using *ab experientia* here [and elsewhere] to mean an experience that he had in the spiritual world and that he recounts in *Arcana Caelestia* §1870'.

[20] At first I translated this as 'True doctrine is *for* those who...', assuming *illis* to be dative; but the first edition of *De Equo Albo* has *ab illis*. Presumably the omission of *ab* from the 1934 Latin text is a slip on someone's part.

[21] Swedenborg's word here is *charitas*: I have pondered long before deciding on 'love in

the sense of affectionate regard', a shade of meaning borne out by the final sentence of paragraph 2 of this section, I think. For fluency I have usually translated this as simply 'love'. 'Charity' is a non-starter these days, and 'dearness' is to me more a synonym for 'expensiveness'.

22 The Latin of our text has *ideae cogitationis* at this point: 'ideas of thought'. Throughout his works Swedenborg often distinguishes between types of ideas but it is self evident in this instance that the ideas referred to are those of 'thought' in opposition to speech and hence *cogitationis* has been dropped.

23 See note 5.

24 The Latin has *descenderat*, pluperfect tense, literally 'had descended'; but the use of the pluperfect for a strong perfect 'is not uncommon in Swedenborg' (Elliott), as is indeed the case sometimes in pre-classical and in poetical Latin. It has been translated as if perfect, therefore.

25 In the end I can find no better word than 'beautiful' for Swedenborg's *pulchra* here. I guess his thought is that the coherent sequence of ideas referred to is pleasing and satisfying, aesthetically and intellectually—hence, 'beautiful' which is the true classical meaning of the word anyway.

26 '*pervaserint totum caelum* (*De Equo Albo*), *impleverint universum coelum* (*De Nova Hierosolyma*). The latter stands closer to what Swedenborg has [...] in the entry in his index which he's drawing on here. On the assumption that *De Equo Albo* is subsequent to *De Nova Hierosolyma*, this exemplifies Swedenborg's continual effort to refine his wording, though I'm not sure why he changed from *impleo* to *pervado*': Elliott, who has noted many similar refinings.

27 'Nearly always, if not always, Swedenborg renders John 1:3 *Omnia per Ipsum*' (Elliott), rather than the *per illud* used here. The form *ipsum* may be either masculine or neuter, enabling through Him as a translation. The current Swedenborg Society editions of *De Equo Albo* and *De Nova Hierosolyma*, however, have *illud* (*it*, neuter), and that is the form I have translated.

28 An interesting glitch has come to light. Both the 1st edition and the 1934 Latin text has [*have*] *viscosa sanguinis*—the sticky/viscous parts of the blood. This may well be a biologically sound concept, but it seemed to me to have nothing to do with Swedenborg's line of thought at this point. Remarking on this to Elliott, I quickly received the reply that *Arcana Caelestia* §5719 has *vitiosa*, 'vicious/sinful': much more satisfactory! It seems that the misreading has been handed down by successive editors for well over 200 years.

29 *Decem verba*, 'Ten Words', is the Latin form of the Hebrew expression which describes the Ten Commandments.

# Index

Amos, 32
ancient book, 32
ancient (representative) churches, 7, 9, 24, 27
ancients, the, 14, 23, 24; ancient folk, 7
angels, 12, 17, 18, 19, 20, 22, 25, 29; angelic ideas, 17; angelic speech, 17
*Arcana Caelestia*, 3, 5, 6, 8, 9
Assembly of the Intelligent and Wise, 7

Balaam, 9
beginning, the, 30
blaspheme, 31
blood, 1, 2, 3, 15, 31
body, 22, 25
bread and wine, 15

Canaan, 24
celestial, 18, 26, 27; angels, 18; kingdom, 18; love, 24
chariots, of Israel, 6; of fire, 7
Christ, 21
Church, the, 3, 4, 5, 10, 12, 13, 14, 15, 21, 23, 24, 26; Jewish, 27; churches, 7, 9; *see also* ancient (representative) churches
contract, 18

correspondence(s), 7, 15, 16, 17, 18, 23, 24, 25
covenant, 18

Dan, 4
Daniel, 32
David, 6, 32
death, 9, 12, 19
Divine, the, 19, 29; divine being, 23; divine providence, 20
doctrine, 6, 7, 13, 14, 21, 22, 28; false, 12; doctrinal ideas, 13, 14, 33

earth, 2, 9, 12, 17, 18, 20, 25; *see also* world
Egypt, 24
Elijah, 6, 7
Elisha, 6, 7
enlightened, enlightenment, 11, 12, 13, 14, 19
Ephraim, 24
Europe, 24
existence, 15, 25
Exodus, 8
external sense, 17, 18, 20, 24, 27; *see also* literal meaning; natural sense

Ezekiel, 32

faith, 3, 10, 12, 13, 14; faithful, 1, 2
false doctrine, 12
fame, 11
flesh, 15, 30
Flood, the, 9
four Evangelists, 32

gain, 11
Genesis, 4, 8, 15, 21
Gentiles, the, 24; gentiles, the, 7
glorification, the, 15, 29
God, 1, 2, 5, 12, 30
god of [Greek] wisdom, 7
god of the sea, 7
Golden Age, 9
Greece, 7, 24; Greek, 13

Habakkuk, 5, 32
Haggai, 32
heaven, 1, 2, 3, 4, 7, 9, 11, 15, 17, 18, 20, 21, 22, 23, 25, 26, 29, 30, 33; heavenly kingdom, 24; heavens, 19
*Heaven and Hell*, 16, 17, 20, 22, 25, 30
Helios, *see* god of [Greek] wisdom
hell, 9, 29
heresies, 28; heresy, 11
historical (parts of the Word), 9, 22, 23
holy, 10, 19, 20, 22, 27; holiness, 11
Holy Supper, 15
honour, 11
horseman, 4, 5, 6
Hosea, 32

inner meaning, 1, 2, 3; innermost sense, 18, 22, 29; inner sense, 4; internal sense, 3, 8, 15, 16, 17, 18, 19, 20, 21, 22, 23, 24, 27, 28, 30, 31, 32, 33; *see also* spiritual sense
internal self, 11; internal being, man, person, 19
Isaiah, 32
Israel, 4, 6, 15, 26, 27
Israelite, 27

Jacob, 15, 24
Jeremiah, 32
Jesus, 21
Jew, 13; Jews, the, 28
Jewish Church, 24, 27
Joash, King, 6
Job, 5, 32
Joel, 32
John, [Revelation], 1; [Gospel], 30, 32
Jonah, 32
Joseph, 24
Joshua, 32
jot and tittle, 10, 20; jot alone, 27
Judah, 15, 24; (house of), 5
judgements, 27
Judges, 32

Kings, Books of, 6, 32
King Joash, 6
King of Kings, 1, 2, 4

Lamentations, 32
law(s), 20, 27
Levi, 24
literal meaning, 2, 3, 20, 21; literal sense, 11, 12, 13, 15, 16, 17, 18, 19, 20, 21, 22, 23, 24, 27, 28; *see also* external sense; natural sense
Lord, the, 2, 3, 4, 5, 6, 9, 10, 11, 12, 13, 14, 15, 18, 19, 20, 21, 22, 23, 24, 26, 29, 30, 33
Lord's Prayer, 20
love, 2, 3, 4, 10, 11, 12, 14, 30, 31, 33; love and faith, 10, 12; love of self, 11, 31; doctrine of love, 14, 21
Luke, 32
madness, 5

## Index

Malachi, 32
Mark, 32
marriage, 21, 29
Matthew, 20, 32
Micah, 32
mock, 5, 31
Moral Theology, 14
Moses, 9, 32
most ancient peoples, 9; most ancient authors, 23
Muses, *see* nine virgins

Nahum, 32
natural, 9, 12, 14, 15, 17, 18, 19, 23, 25, 26, 27, 30; natural sense, 17, 19, 23; *see also* external sense; literal meaning
*New Jerusalem and Its [Heavenly] Doctrine*, The, 9, 14
New Testament, 32
nine virgins, 7

Obadiah, 32
Old Testament, 32
only reality, 29

Pegasus, 7
Peter, 15
Philistines, 14
Poseidon, *see* god of the sea
profanation, profane, 31
Pronouncements, The, 9
prophecies, 9, 15
prophetical (parts of the Word), 4, 5, 9, 15, 20, 21, 22, 32, 33
providence, divine, 20
Psalms, 6, 32
pure in heart, 27

representations, 7, 24, 25; representative, 7, 23, 24, 25, 26, 27
Reuben, 24

revelation, 9, 20
Revelation, Book of, 1, 3, 15, 32; exposition of chapter nineteen, 1-4

sacred, 11
Samuel, Books of, 32
serpent, 4
Simeon, 24
sons of Jacob, The, 24
soul(s), 7, 22, 25
spirits, 18, 25
spiritual, 4, 5, 15, 19, 23, 25; angels, 18; enlightenment, 14; ideas, 11, 12, 17, 19; kingdom, 18; life, 9; perception, 19, 22; realities, 18, 26; speech, 17; things, 15, 27; thinking, 17; truth, 7
spiritual sense, 1, 2, 3, 4, 8, 9, 15, 16, 17, 18, 19, 20, 23, 27; *see also* inner meaning
spiritual world, 6, 21, 25, 30; *see also* world of spirits
statutes, 27
sun, the, 7, 29, 30

Ten Commandments, 20
Ten Words, The 33
three heavens, 19
Trojan Horse, 7
truth, 2, 3, 4, 6, 7, 9, 10, 11, 12, 13, 14, 19, 21, 22, 25, 29, 30, 31, 33

Uncircumcised, the, 14
understanding, 2, 3, 4, 5, 6, 7, 8, 11, 12, 13; understand, 18, 21, 25

virgin, 22; nine virgins, 7

Wars of Jehovah, The, 9
White Horse, 1, 2, 8, 15; white horses, 1, 2, 3
white linen, 1, 2, 3, 4
Word, the 1, 2, 3, 4, 6, 8, 9, 10, 11, 12, 13,

15, 16, 17, 18, 19, 20, 21, 22, 23, 24, 27, 28, 29, 30, 31, 32, 33; historical parts of, 9, 22, 23; list of Books of the Word with internal sense, 32; prophetical parts of, 4, 5, 9, 15, 20, 21, 22, 32, 33
world, 15, 19, 23, 25, 26, 27, 29, 30; *see also* earth
world of spirits, 31; *see also* spiritual world

Zechariah, 5, 32
Zephaniah, 32